NORFOLK COUNTY COUNCIL LIBRARY AND INFORMATION SERVICE
SCHOOL LIBRARY SERVICE - BOOK PURCHASE SCHEME

597
Greer

Newt
WATTS, B.

597.65

withdrawn for sale

SWANTON MORLEY PRIMARY SCHOOL
R03273N5080

ISBN 0 7136 3123 6

Published by A & C Black (Publishers) Limited
35 Bedford Row, London WC1R 4JH

© 1989 Barrie Watts

A CIP catalogue record for this book is available from the British Library

**Acknowledgements**
The illustrations are by Helen Senior
The publisher would like to thank Jennifer Coldrey for her help and advice.

All rights reserved. No part of this publication may be reproduced, stored in a retrieval system, or transmitted in any form or by any means, electronic mechanical, photocopying, recording or otherwise, without the prior permission of A & C Black (Publishers) Limited.

Filmset by August Filmsetting, Haydock, St Helens
Printed in Belgium by Henri Proost & Cie Pvba

# Newt

Barrie Watts

A & C Black · London

# Here is a newt.

Have you ever watched a newt?
You can find them in ponds. Newts can live on land and under water. In winter, newts live under damp stones. They eat worms and small insects.

In spring the newt goes in to the pond to look for a mate.

This book will tell you how a newt comes from a tiny egg.

# The male newt is ready to mate.

Look at the photograph. This is a male newt. He has a flap of skin on his back called a crest. When he is ready to mate, his stomach turns orange.

The male newt has found a female. Her body is full of eggs. The male swims round her. Then he starts to do a dance to attract her.

At first, the female tries to swim away. But after a few days she is ready to mate with the male.

# The newts mate. The female lays her eggs.

The male newt swims backwards and forwards in front of the female. Then he drops a white blob of jelly from his body. The female swims over it and it sticks to her.

Now she is ready to lay her eggs.

Look at the photograph. Can you see how fat the female newt is?

She carefully lays her eggs one at a time on some weed. She sticks each egg to a leaf. Then she folds the leaf over with her back legs to hide the egg.

# Each egg is inside a ball of jelly.

The female newt lays as many as three hundred eggs. It takes her nearly a month.

Look at the photograph. This egg is inside its jelly ball. In the photograph it looks very big. In real life, it is about as big as the top of a match.

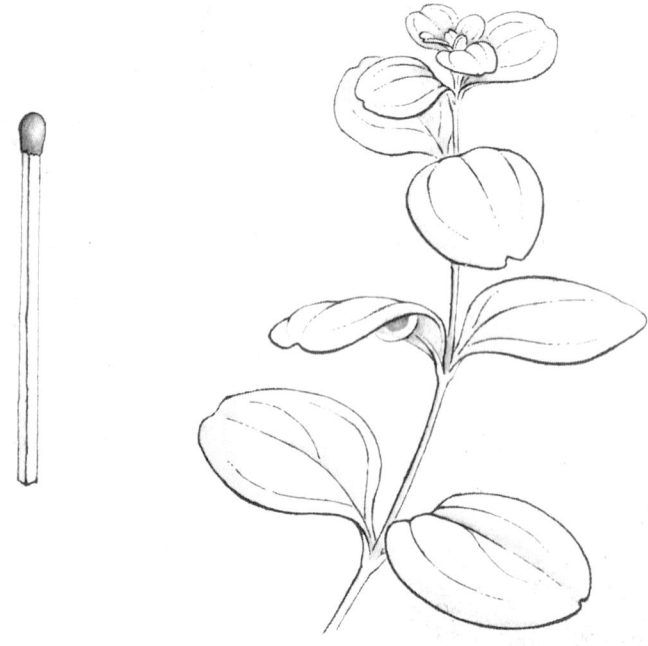

The jelly ball sticks the egg to the plant. Soon the egg starts to change shape.

# The egg changes shape.

After a week the egg has turned white. It has grown longer and is now shaped like a bean.

The outside of the jelly ball begins to look bumpy.

After twelve days the egg begins to look more like a newt. The tail is at the top of the egg and the head is at the bottom. On the young newt's head, there is a bump which will be one of its eyes.

# The young newt hatches.

After sixteen days the egg is twice as big. The newt has a longer tail. The bumps on each side of its head will grow in to gills. They will help the newt to breathe under the water.

This newt is hatching from the egg.

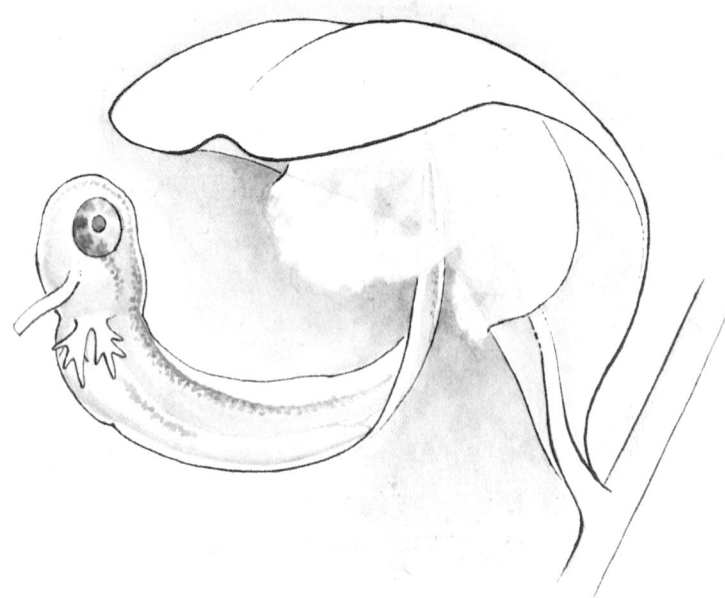

The jelly ball gets softer and the newt wiggles hard to get out.

## The young newt has enemies.

The young newt is called a larva. It has tiny threads under its chin. They are suckers.

The larva cannot swim very well. It sinks to the bottom of the pond. It uses the suckers to stick to a plant.

The young newt has many enemies.

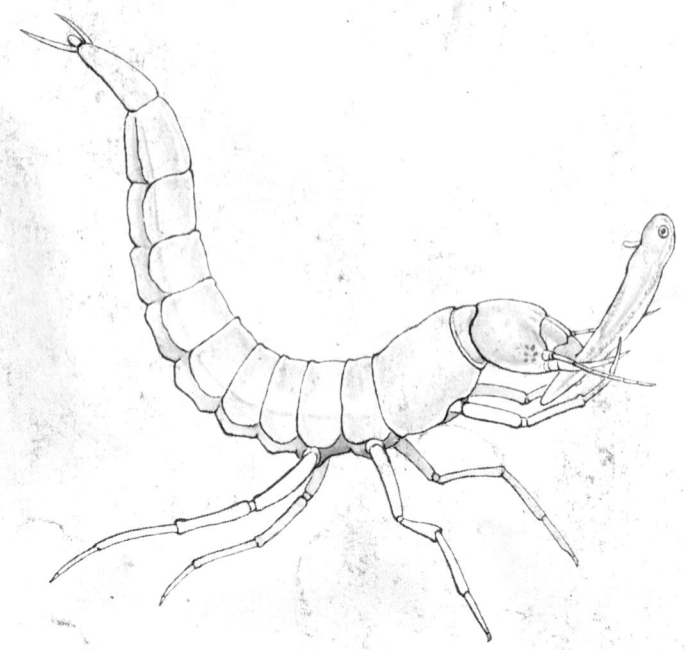

This newt larva is being attacked by a diving beetle.
Lots of young newts are eaten by other pond animals.

# The young newt can breathe under water.

The newt larva is now a week old. It breathes through feathery gills on each side of its head. Look at the photograph. Can you see the young newt's gills?

The young newt eats tiny pond animals all the time and grows bigger.

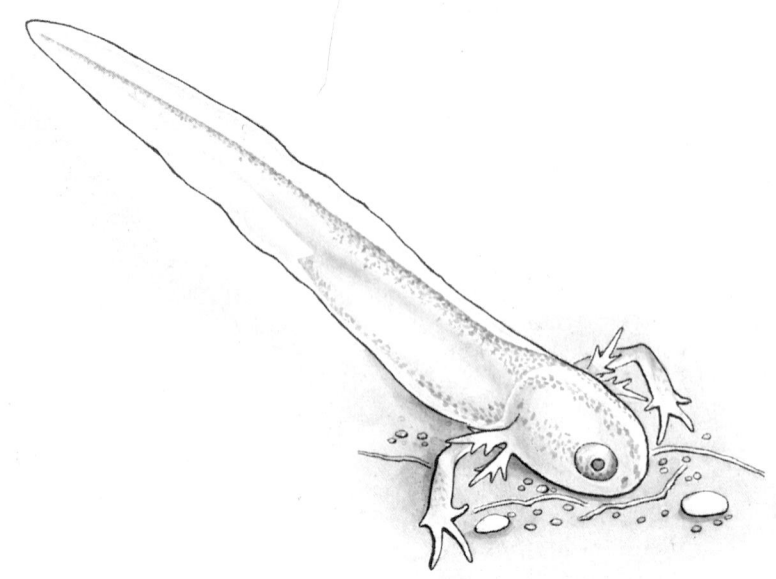

Soon it grows its front legs.

## The young newt grows legs.

The young newt is three weeks old. Look at the big photograph. Its back legs have started to grow. The newt larva can now swim fast by wiggling its tail.

After five weeks the young newt has bushy gills.

The larva begins to look more like an adult newt. It has grown back legs and it can walk along the bottom of the pond to look for food.

Do you remember how a newt came from a tiny egg?
See if you can tell the story in your own words.
You can use these pictures to help you.

## Index

This index will help you to find some of the important words in this book.

breathe  12, 16

eat  2, 14, 16, 20
egg  2, 4, 6, 8, 10, 12
enemy  14

female  4, 6, 8,

gills  12, 16, 18, 20, 22

hatch  12

jelly ball  8, 10

land  2
larva  14, 16, 18
laying  6, 8
legs  6, 16, 18
lungs  20

male  4, 6
mate  2, 4, 6, 22

pond  2, 14, 18, 22

swim  4, 6, 15, 18

tail  10, 12

water  2, 12, 20

Try to find some young newts in a pond. Look for older newts coming to the top of the water to breathe.

25